Publisher and Creative Director: Nick Wells
Project Editor: Polly Prior
Picture Research: Laura Bulbeck
Art Director and Layout Design: Mike Spender
Digital Design and Production: Chris Herbert

Special thanks to: Jane Donovan, Stephen Feather, Karen Fitzpatrick, Michael Heatley

FLAME TREE PUBLISHING

Crabtree Hall, Crabtree Lane
Fulham, London SW6 6TY
United Kingdom

www.flametreepublishing.com

First published 2012

12 14 16 15 13
1 3 5 7 9 10 8 6 4 2

A CIP record for this book is available from the British Library upon request.

ISBN 978-0-85775-522-3

Printed in China

michael bublé

Flying High

MIKE GENT

FOREWORD: RUSTY CUTCHIN, EDITORIAL DIRECTOR,
THE *AMERICAN TUNE TRIBUNE*

**FLAME TREE
PUBLISHING**

Contents

Foreword

Here's a riddle. Who is the hottest singing heartthrob, sells out concert stages all over the world, has won every award in the music business and has recorded scads of songs to which you can have an all-night singalong – with your grandmother?

The honour goes to Michael Bublé, who has proven time and again that a bona fide star can build legions of fans with the classics of yesteryear. But the Canadian crooner also can write a new song with the best of them, as he proved with his international hit 'Haven't Met You Yet'.

As Mike Gent illustrates in this gorgeous volume, few singers have paid the dues and earned the accolades as thoroughly as Michael Bublé. From his salad days touring the Canadian club circuit to his reign at the top of the international charts and in the concert halls, Michael indeed has been flying high.

Just as Frank Sinatra made bobby-soxers swoon and later urged them to come fly with him and swing among the stars, Michael has brought his fans along for the ride, insisting that his ticket prices be affordable, his music accessible and his quality unassailable. He has injected new life into the greatest music of the American and British songbooks, while proving himself the ultimate showman, and perhaps the best hope for keeping our greatest music alive.

But as fans like me know, Michael is no museum piece, no costume drama. He is a star as bright as any in our modern firmament. If there is another talent more deserving of his fame and success, I just haven't met him yet. Who else can make you – and your grandmother – swing and swoon as you fly to the moon?

Rusty Cutchin

Editorial Director, the *American Tune Tribune* (www.tunetribune.com)

Got What It Takes

The Michael Bublé worldwide success story
started in February 2003 when his self-titled debut album
was released. September to December of that year found
him touring in the UK, US, Australia, Singapore, South Africa
and Canada. From March 2004, the Michael Bublé Live in
Concert Tour visited the US, Australia, New Zealand, Ireland
and the UK, ending in December.

In February 2005 his second album, *It's Time*, was released.
Touring recommenced in the US before moving on to
Canada, then back to the States. The tour picked up again
in September in Australia after a month's break. From there
Michael and his band went to the Far East – the Philippines,
Thailand and Indonesia. The *It's Time* roadshow hit Dublin
and Belfast in November 2005 before crossing to the UK
and mainland Europe with dates in the Netherlands, France,
Italy, Germany, Switzerland and Spain. A busy year ended
with a rescheduled gig in Wales.

Niagara To New Mexico

After two dates at Niagara Falls in February 2006, Michael
returned to America for a three-month stint, performing in
23 states. The *It's Time* tour returned to Europe in May to
June for engagements in Luxembourg, France, Germany,

'I'm intolerable. I actually hire someone just to feed me prawn cocktail crisps, one by one. I have to be carried, I don't do stairs any more and I'm also to be called "The Maestro" whenever people are around.'

MICHAEL BUBLÉ

the Netherlands, Denmark, Norway and Sweden before hitting the US again, adding 11 new states to his tally. The tour finished in Albuquerque, New Mexico, in October.

Call Me Irresponsible hit the shops in May 2007, a cue for The Irresponsible Tour to opens in Reno, Nevada, two months later. The first American leg saw Michael playing Las Vegas, Phoenix, Denver, Chicago, New York, Boston and Los Angeles. Europe hosted the next stage of the campaign as the Bublé tour bus stopped at Hamburg, Berlin, Düsseldorf, Munich, Rome, Milan, Florence, Paris, Lyon and Antwerp before ending in the UK. South African performances in Cape Town, Johannesburg and Durban ended the year in sunnier climes.

'You've got girls screaming at you. There are two ways you can handle that – you can take it all in and act like you are that sex symbol, or you can take it with humility and laugh at yourself.'

MICHAEL BUBLÉ

Popular Down Under

North American touring took up the first half of May 2008, with comprehensive coverage of 28 US states before hitting Australia in May. Michael has always been very popular Down Under and completed a month-long stay with gigs in all major cities. Another 10 days of gigs in the UK and Ireland took place in July. The tour returned to the States once again and wound up with a prestigious gig at Madison Square Garden.

The year of 2009 was relatively quiet until *Crazy Love* released in October, The *Crazy Love* Tour kicking off in March 2010 in Orlando, Florida. The first date outside the US was in Sheffield, England, before taking in Italy, Germany, Belgium, Switzerland and France. After more dates in North America, including Canada this time, Michael played to his biggest audience to date, 100,000 people at Dublin's Aviva Stadium, in September. The roadshow flew back to the US to finish the year in Los Angeles.

A Crazy Schedule

February to March 2011 found Michael back Down Under for performances in Brisbane, Sydney, Melbourne, Adelaide and elsewhere. *Crazy Love* arrived in Asia in March, with dates in Singapore, Hong Kong and Malaysia. The tour concluded in the US and Canada in August 2011, while the following March brought shows in South America, Europe and South Africa.

'I need to always keep in my head how lucky I am that I get to have these two hours with these people – I'm fortunate.'

MICHAEL BUBLÉ

It's Time

Producer David Foster was hugely impressed with Michael Bublé as a performer when he signed him to a record deal in 2001, but he had early doubts about how to market the music. However, by the time *Michael Bublé* was released two years later, the climate in the American charts had changed. Mainstream artists were making a comeback, perhaps as a reaction to the domination of the music scene by R&B and rap acts. Singers like Norah Jones and Josh Groban were riding high and selling a lot of records, demonstrating that there was an untapped demand for this kind of music. As luck would have it, Michael was poised to tap into this potential with his major label debut.

'I was never sleazy. I was never mean to a girl. I was always very upfront. But I'm a regular guy. I am a lad and I did enjoy temptation.'

MICHAEL BUBLÉ

With the record company putting its muscle fully behind him, making the promotion of *Michael Bublé* a priority, attention was paid to even the smallest detail. Michael's image was

'People are struggling.
Look at the price of petrol.
I've made more money than
I ever thought I would. I've
sold more albums than
I ever thought I would,
I want people to know I'm not
ripping them off.'

MICHAEL BUBLÉ

upgraded to Armani suits and he was required to forego his beloved Big Macs in order to lose weight and accentuate his George Clooney-like good looks – all this with the target audience of older women in mind.

Getting To Know Him

Radio and, in particular, television were crucial to the success of the album in the US. Appearances at the pre-game Super Bowl show in San Diego, on NBC's breakfast time *Today Show* and the soap opera *Days of Our Lives* were all instrumental in spreading the word.

Michael's combination of the contemporary and the classic, of standards and new songs, is another reason for his phenomenal success. Had he just been a copyist or revivalist, he would not have been nearly as popular with such a wide cross-section of society. As a recording artist, he is committed to delivering something different with each new release, rather than resting on his laurels and repeating the formula of the previous album.

Long Apprenticeship

Live performances are crucial to a singer like Michael and his long apprenticeship saw him hone and perfect his skills in smaller venues. His easy manner with an audience, and the

ease with which he commands the crowds, marked him out early on as a truly gifted showman. Attending a Michael Bublé gig is a special event for fans and, from his earliest days, he has given his all for his audiences.

Although he may have gone along with the record company's strategy to smarten up his appearance, Michael has always been his own man. He remains as down-to-earth as a superstar can be. Part of the reason for this is that his family keep him grounded. They do not allow him to become big-headed and quickly jump on any signs of such behaviour.

Boys, Beer And Hockey

Michael is everyone's elder brother, a young man who likes to drink beer with his buddies and watch ice hockey. He has not led a cosseted existence by going straight from childhood to stardom with nothing in-between. Anyone seeing his appearances on chat shows like *Parkinson* in 2007 could not have failed to be charmed by his self-deprecating good humour and down-to-earth personality.

Having worked for so long to achieve success, Michael has ensured that he has a say in all aspects of his career. There are few stars in his position who would have insisted on lowering ticket prices to an affordable level for the fans, as Michael often has. A nice guy, a gifted singer and a great performer, Michael Bublé is the people's superstar.

'The record business is in trouble. One reason is too many artists put out c**p records on which there are one or two great singles and the rest are fillers.'

MICHAEL BUBLÉ

'Although I like rock 'n' roll and modern music, the first time my granddad played me the Mills Brothers something magical happened. The lyrics were so romantic, so real ... the way a song should be for me.'

MICHAEL BUBLÉ

Under His Skin

It is well known that Michael's grandfather Mitch was one of the biggest influences on his career. He instilled a love of jazz and swing music in his grandson by playing the music of his favourite singers on original vinyl discs.

Michael's earliest musical love was the voice of Bing Crosby, one of the original crooners. Crosby's laidback tones were a great influence on the next generation, notably Frank Sinatra who, like Michael, was of Italian descent. Sinatra needs little introduction, having enjoyed a career that lasted nearly 60 years, mostly at the summit of his profession. His distinctive approach to crooning made him one of the most popular entertainers in the world. Michael has recorded several songs closely associated with Sinatra, notably 'I've Got You Under My Skin' and 'Come Fly With Me'.

That Old Mills' Magic

Less well known to modern audiences but frequently cited by Michael as a fundamental influence are the Mills Brothers, a harmony group whose jazz and straight pop style was immensely popular from 1932 to 1968. They continued to tour with line-up changes into the early 1980s. Bobby Darin was another Italian-American hero of Michael's. He began as a jazz-pop singer, but his later output became more folk-influenced. Darin is best remembered for the self-penned hit 'Dream Lover'; his version of 'Mack the Knife' is regarded as definitive.

Girls On Top

Some of the all-time great female vocalists also influenced Michael. Sarah Vaughan, renowned as one of the best singers of the twentieth century, initially found fame in partnership with the Earl Hines' big band and fellow singer Billy Eckstine before going solo. Often described as a jazz singer, she preferred – like Michael – not to be pigeonholed.

'The cool thing, growing up, (was that) I was listening to the stuff that young people listen to. Pearl Jam and Oasis and Dr. Dre. But it never gave me the real spark that I got listening to Sinatra or Tony Bennett.'

MICHAEL BUBLÉ

Ella Fitzgerald's three-octave range, peerless phrasing and diction saw her hailed as America's First Lady of Song. Her recording career lasted from 1935 to 1989, during which time she became one of the leading interpreters of The Great American Songbook.

Rosemary Clooney, a singer, actress and friend of Frank Sinatra, is also now famous as the aunt of George Clooney! Her early hits were novelty songs but she made a successful career out of more serious jazz in the 1950s.

Crooning Italians

That decade's generation of crooners also form part of the roll call of Michael's influences. Both Tony Bennett and Al Martino are Italian-Americans. Martino branched out into acting, while Bennett survived a career downturn to enjoy renewed popularity in the 1990s and beyond. More firmly in the jazz mould was Mel Tormé, a contemporary of Frank Sinatra. He wrote many songs that have become jazz standards and also acted in movies and television.

Michael's influences were not limited to jazz and traditional pop greats – he enjoyed a greater range of music than most teenagers in the 1980s. Michael Jackson was his biggest idol as a teenager and he has also expressed admiration for the songwriting talents of George Michael.

He learned a valuable lesson from Harry Connick Jr. who, in the late 1980s, demonstrated that there could be a market for contemporary versions of the classic songs of yesteryear. Another of his idols is Stevie Wonder, whose eclectic output showed Michael how performers can avoid being restricted to a single genre. All these diverse influences have played a part in shaping the Michael Bublé of today.

'Listening to Mel Tormé or Ella Fitzgerald or Frank Sinatra as a kid was so great because they had this dulcet tonal quality I hadn't heard in modern singers.'

MICHAEL BUBLÉ

Family Ties

The influence Michael's family had on the development of his career cannot be overstated. He was born on 9 September 1975 in Burnaby, a suburb of Vancouver in British Columbia, Canada. The family were of Italian descent, both sets of grandparents having migrated to Canada. Michael's father, Lewis, was a fisherman who spent weeks away from home on his boat every summer, so Michael and his two younger sisters, Brandee and Crystal, spent a lot of time at their grandparents' house as they helped his mother, Amber, look after the brood.

'Hockey to me is the fastest, most beautiful, intricate game there is. I love it. I love playing it, I love watching it; I eat it, I drink it!'

MICHAEL BUBLÉ

'My grandfather was really my best friend growing up. He was the one who opened me up to a whole world of music that seemed to have been passed over by my generation.'

MICHAEL BUBLÉ

It was here that grandfather Mitch Santagà introduced Michael to the delights of his record collection, which featured jazz and swing music by greats like Frank Sinatra, the Mills Brothers and Bing Crosby, whose album *Merry Christmas*

(1945) – featuring the iconic song 'White Christmas' – was a fixture on the family turntable during the festive season. Michael often reminisces about the many hours he spent with his grandfather listening to a kind of music that had fallen out of fashion in the 1980s. That said, he didn't want to stand out from the crowd as a teenager, so also checked out Guns N' Roses, AC/DC and The Beastie Boys.

A Swinging Christmas

Having fallen in love with jazz and swing, Michael discovered that he possessed a talent for singing it. According to him, this first flowered during a family rendition of 'White Christmas' in the car as they drove home from Mitch's house. As the other voices fell away, the tones that many years later would entrance millions of listeners continued pitch-perfect to the stunned amazement of his parents. Michael says that he inherited his singing skills from his father, who possessed a good voice but could never remember the words. At his grandfather's suggestion, Michael began to learn the old songs that Mitch loved.

As a teenager, Michael might well have assumed that he was destined to follow in his father's footsteps and become a deep-sea fisherman, until the experience of spending three summer vacations on the boat persuaded him otherwise! The work was hard and the conditions hostile and, as the crew sailed north towards Alaska, Michael spent many hours on

'I'd just be ecstatic because Bing Crosby's "White Christmas" would be playing in the house. I drove my parents nuts. Five years old and I listened to that thing through July.'

MICHAEL BUBLÉ

deck wishing he were somewhere else. He whiled away the time listening over and over to mix tapes his grandfather had made for him, learning and absorbing the old-school music. During these trips, he could often be found singing in bars when the ship was in port.

Sport Or Singing?

Michael, like many Canadians, is a passionate devotee of ice hockey, or as it is known in North America, simply hockey. Three generations of Bublé males were fans of the Vancouver Canucks, and Michael and his father were season-ticket holders, religiously attending all the team's home games. If there was one thing the young Michael Bublé loved more than music, it was hockey. He has often lamented that his skills were not sufficient to allow him to make the grade as a professional, or even the school team – but he did represent his high school at the (much less prestigious) game of soccer.

By the age of 15, Michael knew he wanted to be a professional singer. This was not an easy career to follow, but his family supported him all the way. Grandpa Mitch in particular was his grandson's staunchest ally. Michael has often told the now-legendary tale of Mitch offering to do free plumbing work for any club that would allow his grandson to perform there. Little wonder he was destined to make a show business splash …

A Little Fish ...

Although Michael was a natural performer, his stagecraft and showmanship developed over many years of playing in small clubs, singing whenever and wherever he could and learning his trade. His long apprenticeship gave him the confidence and know-how to handle large audiences in the stadiums and arenas of the world.

'I'd be in a strip bar and I'd come onto the microphone and I would say, "Okay, guys, look at how excited you are to see me! You don't want the girls to come by, you want me!"'

MICHAEL BUBLÉ

Anywhere And Everywhere

Michael performing career began modestly, taking his first tentative steps by singing in the high-school canteen. He also sang in shopping malls, on cruise ships and even worked as a singing telegram on Valentine's Day. His grandfather secured

him gigs, but many of them were in venues where the patrons were not necessarily interested in music. Michael was playing strip-joints and seedy nightclubs while still a teenager in high school and it was in these places that he first realized that humour could be a useful weapon in winning over indifferent audiences. He began to develop his banter with the crowd accordingly.

His growing ability to entertain eventually earned him regular gigs, but in the beginning it was far from easy – particularly as his beloved jazz and swing music seemed to have limited appeal and was far from fashionable. Even at this early point in his career, Michael displayed another of the qualities that would be so essential to his success – persistence. He left school at 18 years old with no regular job other than the prospect of long, hard summers on his father's fishing boat. But grandfather Mitch was, as ever, unwavering in his faith, believing in Michael when others began to express doubts about the likelihood of him ever achieving the success he sought.

Keeping The Faith

Michael's perseverance paid off when a victory in a talent contest brought him the first major break of his career at the age of 18. The competition was held in a Vancouver nightclub, The Big Bamboo, and Michael's rendition of the jazz tune 'All Of Me' won him first prize. Things would not prove quite so simple, however. Organizer Beverly Delich,

'I knew that I wanted to do this from an early age. I was always pretty comfortable onstage. I'm actually more comfortable onstage in front of 10,000 people than talking one-on-one with one person.'

MICHAEL BUBLÉ

'I can't tell you how many hours I studied Frank Sinatra or listened to Mel Tormé and visualized myself singing and performing like they did. I even had thoughts like, "What would I say?", "How would I move?" or "What jokes would I tell?"'

MICHAEL BUBLÉ

a local agent and manager, asked Michael his age and when he confessed to being only 18 years old, she was forced to disqualify him because under Canadian law 19 years is the minimum age to gain entry to a nightclub.

Universal Appeal

Nevertheless, Beverly Delich was so impressed with Michael that she invited him to take part in another talent contest. This took place at the Fair at the Pacific National Exhibition in Vancouver, an annual summer event. The judges at this prestigious show were drawn from the city's entertainment and media industries. Delich displayed considerable faith in Michael by arranging for his participation in an already oversubscribed contest. He repaid her with a confident display beyond his years that won him the vocal performance category. Furthermore, singing with a big band in front of a large audience consisting of a mixture of young and old helped reinforce his conviction that his music had across-the-board appeal.

The prize included a tour of Tennessee and the chance to enter a national Canadian talent contest. It was while flying back from Tennessee with Delich that Michael took another important step and asked her to become his manager. She agreed, and his career was poised to enter a new phase – but the sort of major success he craved would prove frustratingly elusive.

Dream On

Michael made his recording debut in 1996 on a six-track disc titled *First Dance,* paid for by his grandfather. The mini-album was not intended for the commercial marketplace, but as a showcase for his talent. He went on to record two full-length albums – *BaBalu* (2001) and *Dream* (2002). These were more professional recordings and released on independent labels.

Following the huge success of his major label debut in 2003, Michael withdrew his independent albums from sale because he was unhappy with the quality of the recordings. This inevitably means they are now in-demand collector's items among the Bublé faithful – particularly *First Dance,* which was circulated largely among family and friends.

BaBalu

BaBalu was a name that held special significance for Michael, belonging both to a jazz song and – more importantly – a downtown Vancouver nightclub where he first established a reputation for himself. Performing in a small, intimate room, he became a star attraction on Sunday and Monday evenings … usually the least well-attended nights. Friends recall one of the secrets of his popularity was to treat each show as if he were headlining at Las Vegas, giving his all every night, irrespective of the size of the audience.

'The audience came to meet a woman or get wasted, but I learned my craft. It taught me how not to reek of desperation, how to step back and try to be charismatic and let them fall in love with me.'

MICHAEL BUBLÉ

Sci-Fi And Skynyrd

Michael never turned down a gig, appearing in clubs all around the Vancouver area. His dedication to duty was such that he was even prepared to appear in red suit and false beard as a singing Father Christmas. Audiences were not always accommodating, however, sometimes pelting him with cigarettes or sarcastically requesting classic rock songs like Lynyrd Skynyrd's 'Freebird'.

Like his youngest sister Crystal who became an actress, Michael was also interested in the non-musical stage. In 1996, he made two appearances in cameo roles in television dramas. The first was in the obscure science-fiction tale *Death Game* (also known as *Mortal Kombat*), the second a marginally larger part in two episodes of the cult show, *The X-Files*.

Playing The King

As the cover of *First Dance* proves, Michael bore a striking resemblance to the young Elvis Presley – and it was this, added to his ability as a vocal mimic, which led to him gaining the role of Elvis in the touring production *Red Rock Diner*. The jukebox musical premiered in Vancouver, then criss-crossed Canada and the US.

One of the other members of the cast, a stunning brunette called Debbie Timuss, helped him with his dancing and soon became Michael's first real love. He went on to appear in another musical revue for the same Vancouver Arts Club

Theatre Company entitled *Forever Swing*, where the music featured was much more up his street.

Moving East

By the turn of the millennium, Michael and Debbie had moved to Toronto, a larger east-coast city that he hoped would provide a bigger stage for him. In some ways, it was like starting all over again, re-establishing himself in the clubs with unfamiliar audiences.

The year 2000 was to be a pivotal one. As he neared his 25th birthday, he began to fear that he would never make it in show business. Small victories, like the use of two songs in the road movie *Here's to Life!* (2000) and a cameo role crooning 'Strangers In The Night' in *Duets*, were not enough to fulfil his ambitions. His faith began to waver and he was on the verge of quitting to take a college course in broadcast journalism.

'The crummy thing was I was making such poor money and I was starting to go into debt. My musicians were getting more than I was.'

MICHAEL BUBLÉ

Just In Time

Michael had been contemplating giving up when manager Beverly Delich persuaded him to give it one more year to see if his hard work of the previous decade could hopefully start to pay off. Reluctantly, and in the absence of any other work, Michael began accepting corporate gigs (parties run by big companies to launch products). To him, these were almost on a par with the strip joints he had performed in, the audiences not particularly interested in listening and reducing him to little more than background noise. Nevertheless, he gave it his all, as usual, and this was to lead to his big break.

According to Michael, this particular gig was to be his last corporate. It would earn him enough money to fly home to Vancouver to take the course in journalism. In the audience was Michael McSweeney, advisor and confidant to former Canadian Prime Minister Brian Mulroney. A fan of jazz and swing, McSweeney was highly impressed by Michael's performance and sought out the singer afterwards to tell him so. On an impulse, Michael gave him the last copy of his *First Dance* CD. He had no idea of McSweeney's connections until his new fan called to tell him that he had played the album to Mulroney, who 'loved it'. This secured Michael an invitation to dine with the Mulroneys, who were so charmed by the singer that they invited him to perform at their daughter's wedding.

'I never sang at a wedding before either. I never wanted to be known as a wedding singer. I sang at one stupid wedding and now I'm the guy who sang at a wedding and got discovered.'

MICHAEL BUBLÉ

'I don't want to be a copycat. What you see is who I am. It's just me and how I grew up, and what I thought was cool. There was always something special about that music to me. I always felt like I was born in the wrong time.'

MICHAEL BUBLÉ

Enter The Hit Man

Held in September 2000, this was no ordinary wedding ceremony, but a lavish affair – the main event in the social calendar of the Canadian capital Ottawa that year. The extravagant celebrations were attended by Jordanian and Yugoslavian royalty, former American president George Bush and erstwhile British Prime Minister Margaret Thatcher, plus a number of American and Canadian media figures.

The day concluded with a party in a lush ballroom in Ottawa. The most important figure in the crowd that night was David Foster. Nicknamed 'the Hit Man' because of his amazing track record, he had produced a who's who of popular music including Chicago, Earth Wind & Fire, Celine Dion, Whitney Houston and Natalie Cole. He had also discovered Irish family group The Corrs, signing them to his own label, 143 Records.

Forewarned by the Mulroney family about Foster's attendance, Michael was not about to let this chance slip. Although similarly primed by Mulroney, Foster was expecting just another wedding singer, but instantly fell under the spell of Michael's irresistible performance. He described Michael hitting the stage 'like a thunderbolt' and how he was 'floored' by a set consisting largely of self-penned songs. Michael recalls performing his show-stopping rendition of the standard 'Mack The Knife', too.

A Shrewd Investment

Although Michael later joked that he 'made it' that night, the road ahead was far from smooth. There was still hard work and tough decisions to come, including parting company with Beverly Delich. And while Foster was a fan of Michael's music, he was uncertain how to market it successfully. Under the terms of the deal first offered, Michael had to find $500,000 to fund the costs of recording. Before the recording of his major label debut began, however, Foster changed his mind and the album was paid for by the record company. The investment would prove a shrewd move.

'I got up on stage and did a bunch of my originals and Foster, I guess, was taken by it. He came up to me and he said "You're pretty good, kid. Do you want to come down to LA next week?" And I thought "Oh my God, I've made it!"' MICHAEL BUBLÉ

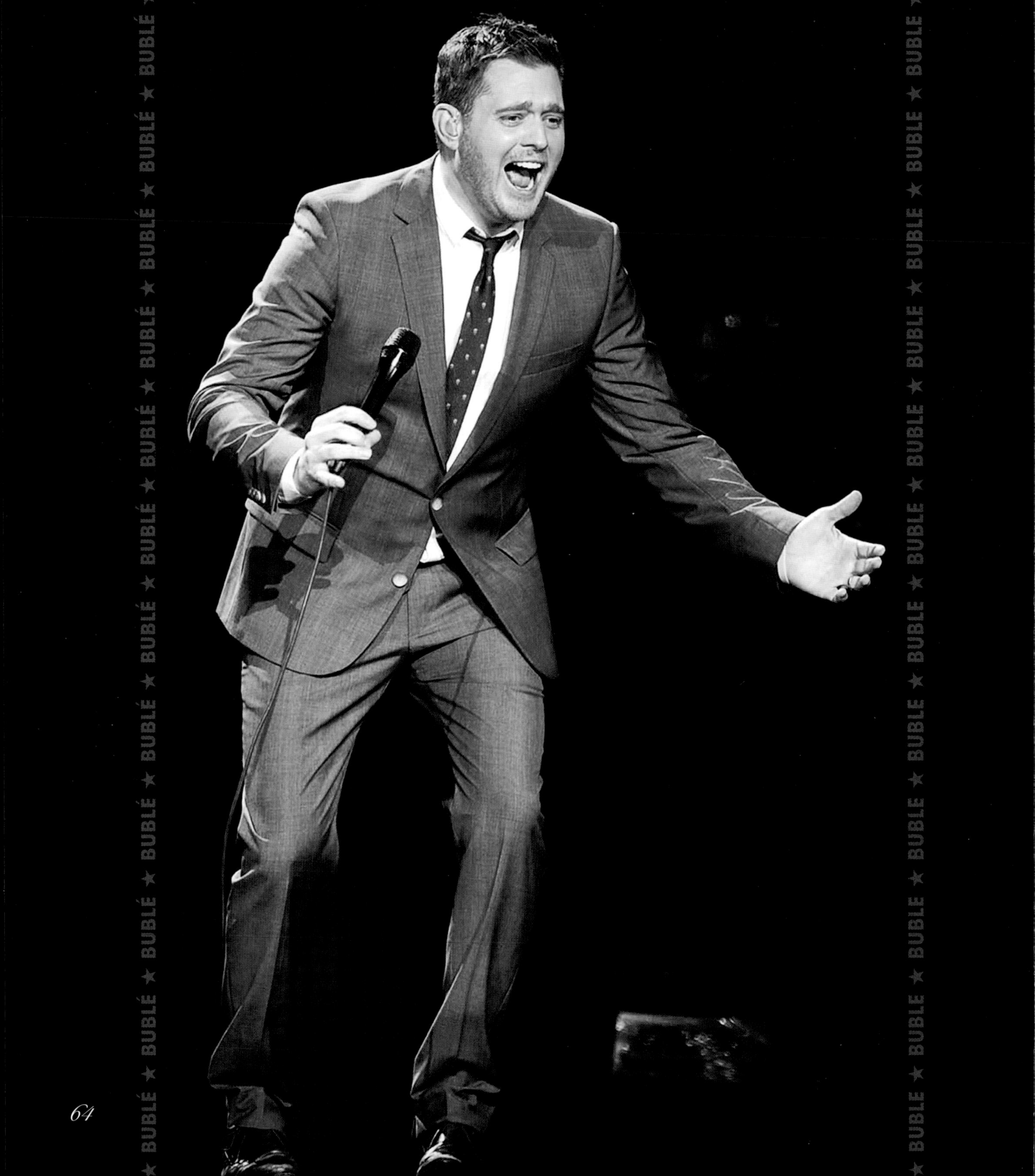

Solid Platinum

Michael Bublé's self-titled debut album was recorded in Los Angeles and Miami Beach over a two-year period from 2001 to 2002 and was finally released in February 2003. A great deal of time and care was taken over the selection of material; both Michael and mentor David Foster were keen to avoid a collection of songs that was backward-looking or might draw accusations of revivalism. Also involved in the tricky task of choosing material was Foster's long-time collaborator and arranger, Humberto Gatica. Foster and Gatica concentrated on standards while Michael delved back into his grandfather's record collection for some less well-known songs.

Ultimately, Michael was happy to let Foster have the final say. What they arrived at was a mix of old and contemporary that created something timeless. The album opened boldly with 'Fever', a song Peggy Lee had made her own in 1958, and included one of Frank Sinatra's most famous calling cards, 'Come Fly With Me', alongside Michael's interpretations of songs by Queen and the Bee Gees. George Michael's 'Kissing A Fool' was perhaps the most surprising choice, but Michael was keen to emphasize that he was an interpreter of great songs from any era.

Success At Home

Michael Bublé was an immediate success in the charts of Michael's native Canada. It sold particularly well in Australia, reaching No. 1, where it was certified seven times platinum.

'We wanted to treat this music with the love and respect it deserves, but the important thing was to capture a spirit and energy and that wasn't confined to any particular musical era.'

MICHAEL BUBLÉ

Equally gratifying were placings in the Billboard Hot 200 albums and the Top 10 in Britain. France, Italy and Sweden also succumbed to the record's charms.

'I'm insecure and my confidence goes back and forth; one day I'm the king, the next I'm a pauper. It's a tough business. It's a slog, but it's work that I love.'

MICHAEL BUBLÉ

'That difficult second album' is a music business cliché, but nevertheless a fair representation of the challenge facing Michael in recording the follow-up to *Michael Bublé* (although strictly speaking, this would be his fourth album!). The dilemma facing the artist is whether to replicate the earlier work and risk being branded predictable or to try something different and risk losing his audience. This time, Michael exerted more control over the choice of songs but did not indulge himself. One of the standout tracks was a Bublé original, 'Home', proving that he was quite capable of writing classic songs himself in collaboration with his creative partners. When released as a single, the song became something of a theme tune for its creator.

Time For A Change

The trust between David Foster and Michael was confirmed when Michael asked to work with another producer on some tracks and Foster immediately agreed. The experienced Tommy LiPuma, who numbered George Benson among his clients, was brought in so that Michael could expand his musical horizons.

Released in February 2005, exactly two years after *Michael Bublé, It's Time* showcased a typically eclectic mix of material. Michael was again unafraid to take on songs associated with others and give them a new lease of life, his version of the Beatles' 'Can't Buy Me Love' and Frank Sinatra's 'I've Got You Under My Skin' are prime examples. Elsewhere, he duetted with fellow Canadian Nelly Furtado on 'Quando, Quando, Quando'.

'The second record is the most important. The first record's easy. The second record is the most important record in an artist's career. Make or break.'

MICHAEL BUBLÉ

Seven Million Sales

Having successfully completed the balancing act between consolidation and innovation, Michael saw the album exceed its predecessor in the US, going Top 10 and eventually being certified triple platinum with three million sales. It topped the charts in Canada and reached No. 5 in the UK. Worldwide sales exceeded seven million. There could no longer be any doubt – Michael Bublé was a major figure in the music business across the world.

Swinging Success

For the follow-up to *It's Time*, Michael had to deal with a new pressure – the weight of expectation, added to the need to please his public and his desire to grow as an artist. He now involved himself in all aspects of production, from choosing the songs to attending the mastering sessions, something almost unheard of for a singer like him. The result emerged as *Call Me Irresponsible* in May 2007. Perhaps the most eagerly awaited aspect of the new album was the inclusion of two new Bublé originals, 'Everything' and 'Lost' – which, like 'Home', drew on his own experiences. He described 'Lost' as 'an anthem for star-crossed lovers'.

As on his previous two major label albums, Michael tackled a song closely associated with Frank Sinatra. However, 'The Best Is Yet To Come' was also sung by, and originally written for, another of his heroes, Tony Bennett. A more leftfield cover version was 'Me And Mrs Jones', the Philly soul classic made famous by Billy Paul in 1973. Michael added a female voice, supplied by girlfriend, the actress Emily Blunt. Equally unpredictable was the choice of Leonard Cohen's 'I'm Your Man', showing once more the breadth of Michael's musical knowledge and his passion for great songs.

Crazy Chart Topper

When *Call Me Irresponsible* went straight in at No. 2 in the Billboard charts and rose to the top slot the following week,

'At no point have I celebrated the success of the last two records and nor will I celebrate the success of this one, if it's successful. The second it comes out I'll go to work, I'll tour. And my mind is already on the next record; coming up with great ideas.

MICHAEL BUBLÉ

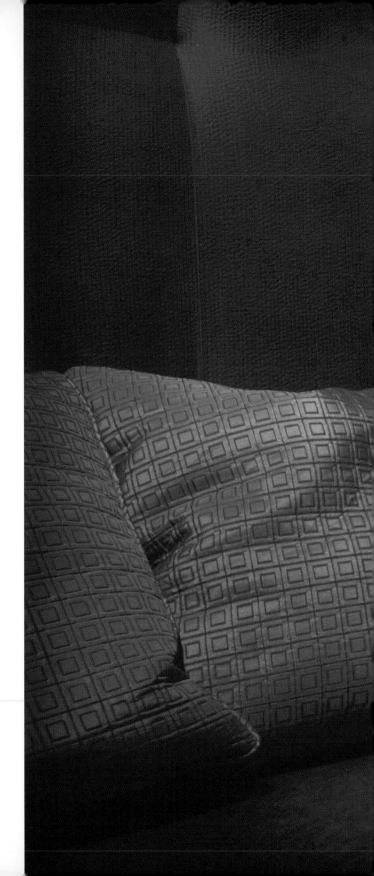

Michael joined an elite group of artists, including his boyhood idol Michael Jackson, who had achieved that feat. Two million sales were racked up in the US alone and the album proved equally popular around the world, particularly Australia where it became the best-selling album of 2007.

The phenomenal chart performance of *Call Me Irresponsible* was exceeded by its successor, *Crazy Love* (2009), as Michael's worldwide popularity grew, thanks to his hard work in promoting his music by tours and personal appearances. *Crazy Love* hit the stores in October 2009 and immediately achieved the rare feat of debuting at No. 1 in the US. UK sales accounted for two of an amazing nine million across the globe.

'David Foster's a genius like I'll never be but his instinct is to play safe, give the audience what they know they want. I want to take it to another level: growth without alienation. If we just keep giving them the same thing, why will they keep buying it?'

MICHAEL BUBLÉ

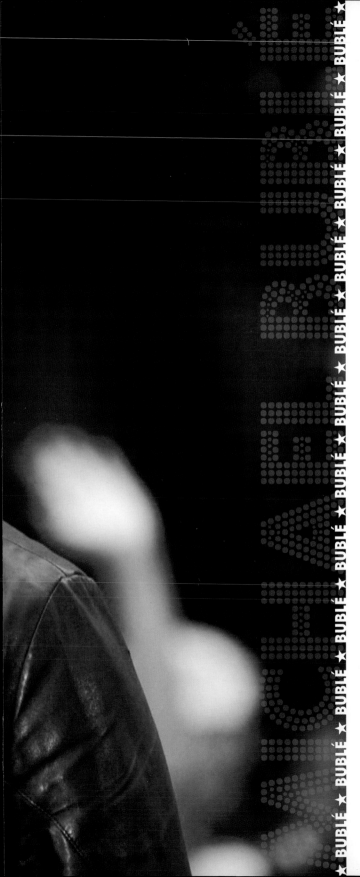

A Smooth Operator

Although Michael! would rightly protest at being described as a revivalist, there is no doubt that he has helped spark renewed interest in the music which he loves above all else – jazz and swing, the big-band sound and traditional pop.

Jazz is a term that embraces various different but related styles. It first became popular as ragtime around the turn of the twentieth century; the 1920s and 1930s are commonly known as the Jazz Age. Swing music, as played by big bands usually consisting of 17 or more musicians, was established by 1935. Bandleaders like Count Basie, Duke Ellington and Tommy Dorsey were among its most popular performers. Swing differed from jazz in its use of a rhythm section consisting of drums and double bass, which provided a solid foundation for the brass section.

Fronting The Band

Bandleaders often employed singers who would go on to enjoy successful singing careers in their own right: Frank Sinatra was Tommy Dorsey's most famous protégé. The popularity of these crooners, who sang standard pop songs, had supplanted swing as the US's most popular music by the mid-1940s. Crooning was a more intimate style of singing that emerged as a direct result of the invention of the microphone. Generally, crooners were backed by a big band, an orchestra

'I love reinterpreting these great standards. There's a reason why some of these songs are 90 years old and people still know them: they talk about things that are always going to be relevant: love and loneliness and betrayal.'

MICHAEL BUBLÉ

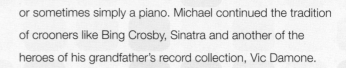

or sometimes simply a piano. Michael continued the tradition of crooners like Bing Crosby, Sinatra and another of the heroes of his grandfather's record collection, Vic Damone.

Singers like Perry Como and Mel Tormé remained at the forefront of popular music until the middle of the 1950s when the focus shifted to rock'n'roll. Anything predating the advent of this genre is now referred to as traditional pop, while classic tunes from the pre-rock'n'roll era come under the umbrella term of The Great American Songbook. This is something Michael has frequently dipped into: 'That's All', 'The Way You Look Tonight' and 'I've Got the World on a String' just three examples. But he is as much a fan of Elvis Presley as Bing Crosby, and his tastes are not restricted to any era.

Two's Company

The duet is a tradition Michael proudly continues, often springing surprises with his choice of singing partners. In addition to the appearance of then-girlfriend Emily Blunt on 'Me And Mrs Jones', *Call Me Irresponsible* featured two other duets. On 'Comin' Home Baby' Michael sang with R&B band Boyz II Men, while his interpretation of Eric Clapton's 'Wonderful Tonight', a long-time personal favourite, showcased guest vocalist Ivan Lins – a highly respected Brazilian singer and songwriter whose work has been covered by many artists. In addition to the duet with Nelly Furtado on 'Quando, Quando, Quando', *It's Time* also featured a guest appearance by jazz-pop fusion trumpeter Chris Botti on 'A Song For You'.

Two By Two

Crazy Love contained three eclectic duets. Acappella group Naturally 7, who also use their voices to mimic instruments, appeared on 'Stardust', while soul funk revivalists Sharon Jones and The Dap-Kings ripped it up with Michael on 'Baby (You've Got What It Takes)'. Third and last came the bonus track, a duet with Ron Sexsmith on his song 'Whatever It Takes'. *Christmas* found room for guest slots featuring British vocal harmony trio The Puppini Sisters, fellow Canadian Shania Twain and Mexican chanteuse Thalia.

Traditional pop, jazz, swing, rock'n'roll and R&B are all part of the musical mix that goes to make the unique sound of Michael Bublé.

'I know who I am and what my personal style is and it doesn't matter to me whether a song was written in 1930 by George Gershwin or by George Michael in 1991.' MICHAEL BUBLÉ

'There will never be another Frank Sinatra. I never wanted to be another Frank Sinatra. I only wanted to be another Michael Bublé.'

MICHAEL BUBLÉ

'I was so scared that I had spent so much time trying to make it that I had come too far. It was either I need to do I don't know what, or quit. I was 26 years old and I had no money, and I wanted to have kids one day.'

MICHAEL BUBLÉ

Chocolate For The Ears

Michael Bublé is classed as a baritone, although this description is not particularly helpful as most non-classical male singers are also baritones. The rich and easy timbre of his voice, especially at the lower end of his range fits the profile, although he is equally comfortable with higher notes more usually associated with a tenor. Some would describe Michael's voice as a lyric baritone, having a smoother, lighter and mellower quality than other singers in the category.

Anyone who has heard his independent albums will testify to the improvement in Michael's singing since they were recorded. His voice is lower now, a factor he attributes largely to age and a natural deepening of the vocal chords.

A Shore Thing

From his early teens it was evident that Michael had a promising voice, ideally suited to the kind of music he loved: jazz and swing. Natural ability is one thing, but it takes work to develop talent and he was always aware that practice was needed to turn that into something special. Even the most gifted singers require coaching and, when Michael was still a teenager, his grandfather paid for him to take singing lessons from Joseph Shore, a well respected operatic baritone.

The Showman

The house lights dim; behind the curtain, silhouettes of a band can be seen. To screams and cheers, Michael Bublé starts singing 'Cry Me A River' before he slowly emerges on to the stage wearing his familiar black suit, white shirt and black tie. A single spotlight shines on him. The big auditorium, a sports arena filled with 10,000 or more people is transformed into an intimate Las Vegas nightclub from the 1950s, complete with 13-piece swing band, revealed when the curtain falls.

The remarkable transformation is partly achieved by lighting – but the main reason is Bublé the showman, whose charisma fills the big spaces, which his popularity enables him to play. Throughout his live shows, Michael keeps up a constant dialogue with the audience, but he isn't talking 'at' them. He has an uncanny ability to connect with the largest of crowds; he opens up, telling stories about his life and how his grandfather influenced him. He thanks the fans for their support with real sincerity.

Intimate Conversation

Michael cracks jokes with self-deprecating humour. Referring to his recent marriage during the 2011 tour, to a wave of booing from the female fans, he responded: 'Great! Half of the

arena is booing me, and the other half is husbands and boyfriends saying "I don't care if he IS married … I still think Bublé's gay!"' This is a regular Bublé joke, but the irony is that Michael inevitably ends up charming even the most recalcitrant male audience members.

The sense of intimacy is reinforced when Michael sits at the edge of the stage and talks to individual audience members. He reads out banners, invites people to have photos taken with him, hugs them, wishes someone happy birthday. He has even been known to invite fans on stage to sing with him.

Up Close And Personal

During the 2011 tour, Michael would leave the main stage and walk through the audience, singing all the while, on his way to a small stage at the rear of the arena. Not only do a lot of fans get to see their idol close up, but for the space of a few songs at least, the worst seats in the house become the best.

After spending so many years playing nightclubs and struggling to make ends meet before finding success, Michael could have been forgiven for disapproving of the instant route to success provided by the likes of *X Factor* and *American Idol*. In reality, he would have been only too pleased to have kick started his career that way. Michael appeared in the 2009 series of *X Factor* as a celebrity mentor, a task that included

'This has been my dream – if I could give you a gift it would be for everyone of you to be on the stage to see what this feels like.'

MICHAEL BUBLÉ

'I would have gone on Pop Idol. I would have done anything to make it. I was on the club circuit for ten years and on the verge of giving up.'

MICHAEL BUBLÉ

an unlikely duet with Essex girl Stacey Solomon on 'Feeling Good'. He was smart enough to realize that appearing on such a popular television show would help raise his profile in the UK. Michael returned to perform on the series finale in 2011, promoting his *Christmas* album.

A Fond Farewell

Back in the sports arena, the show is drawing to an end. Michael kicks monogrammed beach balls from the stage; they are bounced around by the crowd and confetti falls from the rafters. The performance concludes with 'Song For You', the final encore, during which Michael sings unaccompanied, without a microphone, his pure voice alone filling the arena. Then he is gone.

'I'm so excited and so terrified at the same time. I don't want people to hate it. I want them to love it. Every artist's nightmare is to be in the "whatever happened to?" file.'

MICHAEL BUBLÉ

Well-Liked

The internet and social media are essential tools for any artist to promote their work and furthermore they allow fans to communicate with each other to an extent previously undreamt of. Not surprisingly, Michael Bublé has a significant presence in cyberspace; there are hundreds of Facebook pages bearing his name and the official one boasts over five million 'likes'.

His official website, www.michaelbuble.com, is a well-managed and comprehensive operation, regularly updated and a must for the devoted Bublé fan to keep in touch with their idol's activities. The site offers worldwide shopping facilities, too. In addition, there is the official online fan club, www.bungalow-b.com, which offers various levels of membership.

'I don't have much in common with the Rat Pack. I don't wear a tuxedo; I don't drink martinis. I'm happier with a Game Boy than a cigar.' MICHAEL BUBLÉ

Friendly Fanatics

The official site has also played a large part in building a community of fans. The forums on his website confirm that Bublé fanatics love to discuss every aspect of Michael's life and career, swap information and post photographs of themselves with their idol. What's more, unlike many internet forums, the atmosphere is welcoming and friendly; there is a very real sense of camaraderie here.

Recognizing the power of the internet and social forums like Facebook and Twitter, Michael has used them to his advantage. Shortly before the release of *Crazy Love* in 2009, he teased fans by leaking out small pieces of information about the album on Facebook and on *The Daily Bublé*, the online newspaper of his official site.

Staying Connected

From his very earliest days singing in the clubs of Vancouver, Michael has sought to establish a rapport with his audience. He is aware that the connection does not end the moment he walks off stage and that it takes attention to detail and hard work to keep millions of fans happy. After each gig, Michael is happy to sign autographs and pose for photos with fans. Although it can be a daunting experience to come face to face with an idol, Michael remains approachable and charming, skilled at making nervous fans feel at ease.

'It is nice for me to speak about my own personal life in front of the audience; I think it makes me a lot less predatory as an entertainer.'

MICHAEL BUBLÉ

It might have been expected that marriage would have affected his relationship with his female devotees, but this would not seem to be the case. There was no outbreak of jealousy directed at Luisana Lopilato when she and Michael tied the knot in March 2011. His female admirers were generally happy for him and wished him good luck via the online forums, although the messages were tinged with sadness that he was no longer 'available'.

Brits Forever!

As a Canadian, Michael naturally feels a great sense of kinship with his British fans, who accepted and welcomed him immediately. He admits that the connection is party based on the fact that both nationalities share common ground – they are not Americans! Michael has many champions in the British media including chat show host and radio DJ Michael Parkinson, presenter Dermot O'Leary and, more unexpectedly, comedian Peter Kay, who took his grandmother to a gig and, against his expectations, was immediately won over.

There is a common misconception that Michael Bublé's fans are mainly female. Michael himself has played up to this, often joking that the only men in the audience have been cajoled into attendance by their wives and girlfriends. In fact, his appeal crosses the generations and genders. While it is true to say that many of his most passionate followers are female, his talent, impeccable choice of material and exemplary showmanship guarantee any sceptics in the crowd at a Bublé performance will be converted. Just ask Peter Kay!

'I studied all the vocalists – I'm not a jazz guy. I'm a pop singer in the traditional sense where I'm singing pop standards and popular songs of today.'

MICHAEL BUBLÉ

'I wouldn't be happy singing all originals. It's just not me. Maybe that'll bite me on the butt, but my passion is interpreting the greatest songs ever written.'

MICHAEL BUBLÉ

Reaping The Awards

Even before his commercial breakthrough, Michael had been nominated for two Genie Awards in 2001, the Canadian version of the Oscars, for the two original songs that he contributed to the soundtrack of the movie *Here's To Life!*: 'I've Never Been in Love Before' and 'Dumb Ol' Heart'. Sadly, neither won the category. Since then, he has been nominated for and won numerous awards in his native Canada, the US and beyond.

Not surprisingly, his major label debut featured strongly in the 2004 Juno Awards, Canada's equivalent of the Grammies. Michael carried away the trophy for Best New Artist and was an unsuccessful nominee for Album of the Year for *Michael Bublé*.

Top Of The World

In 2005, Michael's growing popularity was confirmed when he won a World Music Award. These are based on certified figures by the International Federation of the Phonographic Industry. Michael was named World's Best Selling Artist/Canada.

The following year saw him make a clean sweep of the Junos. *It's Time* was named Pop Album of the Year and Album of the Year, 'Home' was Single of the Year and Michael was crowned Artist of the Year. Also in 2006, *It's Time* won a German Echo award for Jazz Production of the Year and was nominated for a Grammy.

BUBLÉ ★ BUBLÉ ★ BUBLÉ ★ BUBLÉ ★ BUBLÉ ★ BUBLÉ ★ BUBLÉ ★ BUBLÉ ★ BUBLÉ ★

It would take two more years before Michael carried away perhaps the most prestigious award in the world of music. The Grammy he sought finally came his way in 2008 when *Call Me Irresponsible* was voted Best Traditional Pop Vocal Album.

'I'm not in the record business. This is not about CDs, this is about creating a brand name – putting on a great show so that when the next album comes out, people will be excited to hear what I've done next.'

MICHAEL BUBLÉ

A Fan Favourite

The 2008 Junos were not quite so kind to Michael as in 2006, with him winning only one of the five nominations. He could, however, take consolation in that his sole success was in winning the Fan Choice Award, which had eluded him on two

'I have a **real** **strong** **feeling** that, if you **keep giving** people the **same thing**, they'll go, "**Honey**, I've got **four Bublé albums**, we don't need another."'

MICHAEL BUBLÉ

previous occasions. The same year saw him presented with two Canadian Smooth Jazz Awards for Best Male Vocalist and Best Original Composition for 'Everything'.

Another Grammy found its way to his mantelpiece in 2010 as the live album *Michael Bublé Meets Madison Square Garden* (2009) triumphed in Best Traditional Pop Vocal Album category. A Brit Award continues to elude Michael, however. He was an unsuccessful nominee for Best International Male Solo Artist in 2010, as he had been two years earlier.

Junos And Grammies

The 2010 Juno Awards was another field day for Michael. He won Pop Album of the Year and Album of the Year with *Crazy Love*, Single of the Year for 'Haven't Met You Yet' and the Fan Choice Award. He also received nominations for Artist of the Year and Songwriter of the Year. The American Music Awards were instituted as an alternative to the Grammies and are voted for by the public rather than the music industry. Michael was delighted to win his first such award in 2010, the vote for Favorite Adult Contemporary Artist.

The statuettes continued to come his way. The year 2011 brought a third Grammy, this time for *Crazy Love*, which was adjudged Best Traditional Pop Vocal Album. 'Haven't Met You Yet' was nominated for, but did not win, the Best Male Pop Vocal Performance category.

Marriage And Beyond

Breaking the hearts of his female fans around the world, Michael Bublé finally tied the knot on 31 March 2011 when 23-year-old Argentinean actress Luisana Lopilato became his bride. The couple actually had three ceremonies. The first, a civil one in Buenos Aires, was followed by a larger event in the city for 300 guests and then another party in Michael's native Vancouver for 500 attendees. The couple did not go on a lavish honeymoon, flying instead to Africa to do some work for children's charities. Michael had previously been engaged to English actress Emily Blunt but the pair split up in 2008. Before that, his other long-term girlfriend was Debbie Timuss, a dancer/actress he met in his pre-fame days.

Fatherhood Beckons?

Michael first encountered Luisana, the star of Argentina's most popular soap opera, in November 2008 when they were introduced by the head of his Argentinean record company. A year later, Michael asked her to marry him. Given his strong belief in family values, it seems only a matter of time before he becomes a father. Having almost quit singing back in 2001 because he wanted to raise a family, parenthood looks inevitable for Michael and his lovely wife. He has already started joking about names for the babies, with Bella Bublé mentioned as a possibility!

'I'm a boy, I didn't grow up thinking about my wedding day, so for me, I just want it to be good for Luisana. Really, I just want her to feel like she's had the perfect day.'

MICHAEL BUBLÉ

A Giant Sports Fan

Ice hockey remains one of Michael's passions, to the extent that his rider for gigs stipulates that there must be a local ice-hockey team puck in his dressing room for each gig. Still a committed fan of the Vancouver Canucks, he is also the co-owner of the Vancouver Giants, a successful junior ice-hockey outfit. He shares his stake in the team with his father.

Michael's other interests outside music include an investment in the Tsawwassen Golf & Country Club. Tsawwassen, which means 'looking towards the sea', is situated on the British Columbian coast not far from Vancouver. The facility was closed for refurbishment at the end of 2011 and the five-year project will result in an improved golf course, apartments and houses, plus a spa and gym.

Staying At The Top

With dates in South America, Europe and South Africa, the expectation of a new album in 2012 was raised, hot on the heels of the hugely successful *Christmas*. The evolution of his music will undoubtedly continue as he revisits The Great American Songbook and surprises fans with cleverly chosen cover versions of more contemporary songs as well as finely crafted original music. Having worked so long and hard to get to the top, Michael Bublé intends to remain there.

'I'll continue to keep doing what I was built to do – interpret the greatest songs that were ever written and to try and write some of my own that can try their best to match up to those great ones.'

MICHAEL BUBLÉ

Further Information

Michael Bublé Info

Birth Name   Michael Steven Bublé

Birth Date   9 September 1975

Birth Place   Burnaby, BC, Canada

Height   1.77 m (5 ft 10 in)

Nationality   Canadian

Hair Colour   Brown

Eye Colour   Blue

Discography

Albums

First Dance (1995)

BaBalu (2001)

Dream (2002)

Michael Bublé (2003)

Come Fly With Me (Live, 2004)

It's Time (2005)

Caught In The Act (Live, 2005)

Call Me Irresponsible (2007)

Michael Bublé Meets Madison Square Garden (Live, 2009)

Crazy Love (2009)

Christmas (2011)

EPs

First Dance (1995)

Totally Bublé (2003)

Let It Snow! (2003)

More (2005)

With Love (2006)

A Taste of Bublé (2006)

Special Delivery (2010)

Hollywood: The Deluxe EP (2010)

A Holiday Gift For You (2010)

Singles *(selected)*

2004:   'Spider-Man Theme' (Canada No. 6)

2005   'Feeling Good'

   'Home'